GAME DAY: FOOTBALL

LINEBACKERS

By Jim Gigliotti

Reading consultant: Cecilia Minden-Cupp, Ph.D.,
Literacy Specialist

Gareth Stevens
Publishing

Please visit our web site at www.garethstevens.com.
For a free catalog describing Gareth Stevens Publishing's list of high-quality books, call 1-800-542-2595 (USA) or 1-800-387-3178 (Canada). Gareth Stevens Publishing's fax: 1-877-542-2596

Library of Congress Cataloging-in-Publication Data
Gigliotti, Jim.
    Linebackers / by Jim Gigliotti.
        p. cm. — (Game day. Football)
        Includes bibliographical references and index.
    ISBN-10: 1-4339-1959-1 — ISBN-13: 978-1-4339-1959-6 (lib. bdg.)
    1. Linebackers (Football)—United States—Juvenile literature.
    2. Linebackers (Football—United States—Biography—Juvenile literature. I. Title.
GV951.18.G54 2009
796.332'24—dc22   2009006802

This edition first published in 2010 by
Gareth Stevens Publishing
A Weekly Reader® Company
1 Reader's Digest Road
Pleasantville, NY 10570-7000 USA

Copyright © 2010 by Gareth Stevens, Inc.

Executive Managing Editor: Lisa M. Herrington
Senior Editor: Brian Fitzgerald
Senior Designer: Keith Plechaty

Produced by Q2AMedia
Art Direction: Rahul Dhiman
Senior Designer: Dibakar Acharjee
Image Researcher: Kamal Kumar

Photo credits
Key: t = top, b = bottom, c = center, l = left, r = right
Cover and title page: David Stluka/Getty Images.
Mike Zarrilli/NFL/Getty Images: 4–5; NFL/Getty Images: 6; Pro Football Hall of Fame/NFL Photos/Getty Images: 7; Frank Rippon/NFL/Getty Images: 8; Robert Riger/Getty Images: 9; Kidwiler Collection/ Diamond Images/Getty Images: 10; Mike Powell/Allsport/Getty Images: 11; Vernon Biever/NFL Photos/ Getty Images: 12; Kidwiler Collection/Diamond Images/Getty Images: 13; Focus on Sport/Getty Images: 14, 15; George Gojkovich/Getty Images: 16; Andrew D. Bernstein/Getty Images: 17; Scott Boehm/Getty Images: 18; Jonathan Daniel/Getty Images: 19; Paul Spinelli/Getty Images: 20, 21; Michael Zagaris/Getty Images: 22; Larry French/Getty Images: 23; Donald Miralle/Getty Images: 24; David Stluka/Getty Images: 25; David Drapkin/Getty Images: 26; Paul Jasienski/Getty Images: 27; Bill Baptist/Getty Images: 28; Grant Halverson/Getty Images: 29; Dilip Vishwanat/Getty Images: 30; Paul Jasienski/Getty Images: 31; Rob Tringali/Sportschrome/Getty Images: 32; Harry How/Getty Images: 33; Al Bello/Getty Images: 34; Rob Tringali/Sportschrome/Getty Images: 35; Stephen Dunn/Getty Images: 36; Paul Spinelli/Getty Images: 37; Scott Boehm/Getty Images: 38, 39; Mike Eliason: 40, 41, 42, 43; Jed Jacobsohn/Allsport/Getty Images: 44; George Gojkovich/Getty Images: 45.
Q2AMedia Art Bank: 9cl, 19tl

Printed in the United States of America

CPSIA Compliance Information: Batch#CR909011GS: For further information contact Gareth Stevens, New York, New York at 1-800-542-2595

Cover: Brian Urlacher of the Chicago Bears is one of the top linebackers in pro football.

Contents

Words in the glossary appear in **bold** type the first time they are used in the text.

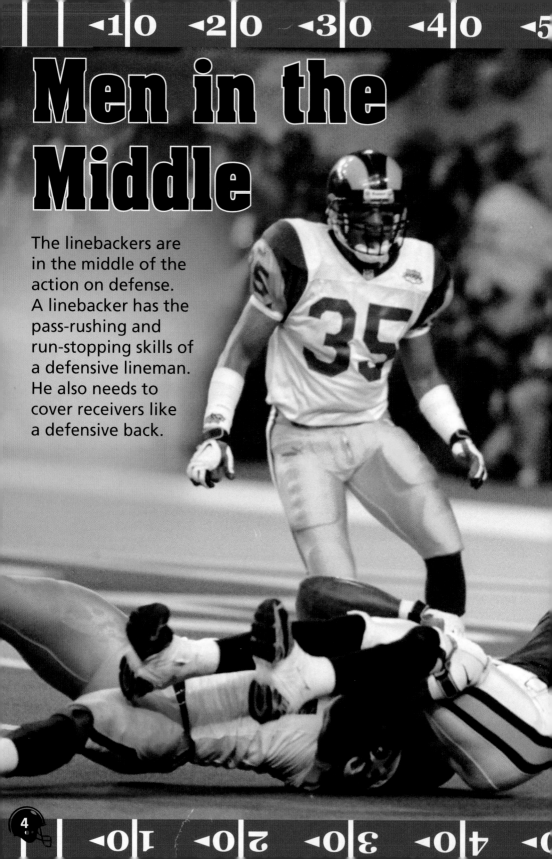

Men in the Middle

The linebackers are in the middle of the action on defense. A linebacker has the pass-rushing and run-stopping skills of a defensive lineman. He also needs to cover receivers like a defensive back.

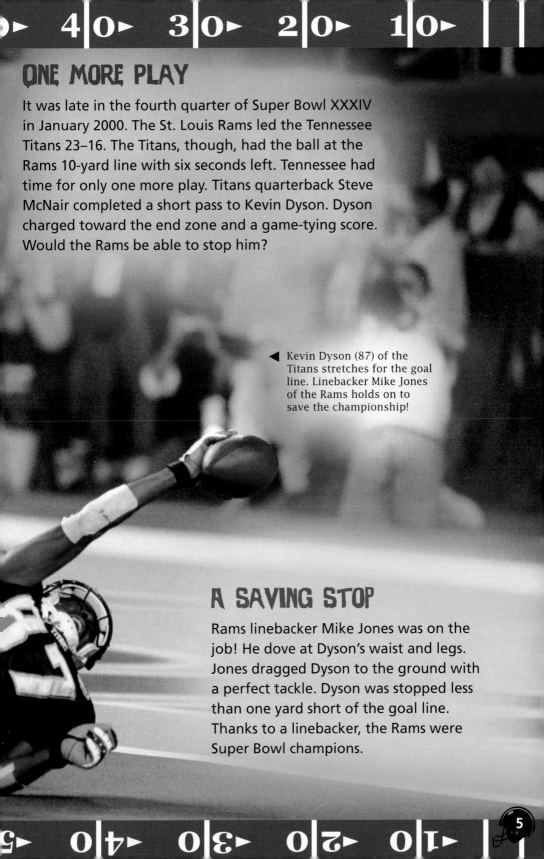

ONE MORE PLAY

It was late in the fourth quarter of Super Bowl XXXIV in January 2000. The St. Louis Rams led the Tennessee Titans 23–16. The Titans, though, had the ball at the Rams 10-yard line with six seconds left. Tennessee had time for only one more play. Titans quarterback Steve McNair completed a short pass to Kevin Dyson. Dyson charged toward the end zone and a game-tying score. Would the Rams be able to stop him?

◄ Kevin Dyson (87) of the Titans stretches for the goal line. Linebacker Mike Jones of the Rams holds on to save the championship!

A SAVING STOP

Rams linebacker Mike Jones was on the job! He dove at Dyson's waist and legs. Jones dragged Dyson to the ground with a perfect tackle. Dyson was stopped less than one yard short of the goal line. Thanks to a linebacker, the Rams were Super Bowl champions.

CHAPTER 1

Linebacker History

Today, almost all defensive **formations** include three or four linebackers. But back when the National Football League (NFL) began in 1920, defenses had only two linebackers. As offenses changed, the linebacker position changed, too.

▼ Even in early football, the defense had the same job it has today: Stop the player with the ball!

EARLY FOOTBALL GAMES

Early in the 1900s, football games included a lot of running plays and big pileups. Over and over, players smashed together at the **line of scrimmage**. Offenses usually just ran the football and advanced it slowly up the field. Defenses tried to stop them by putting nine men on the line. It was a game of brute strength, with one man squaring off directly against another.

THE GAME CHANGES

As offenses began to throw the ball more, defenses had to adjust. They had to cover receivers and protect more of the field. The nine-man front line became an eight-man front. Then a seven-man front. Then six, then five. By the 1940s, most teams played with five defensive linemen and two linebackers. The linebackers were positioned on the ends of the defensive line. The other four defenders were defensive backs.

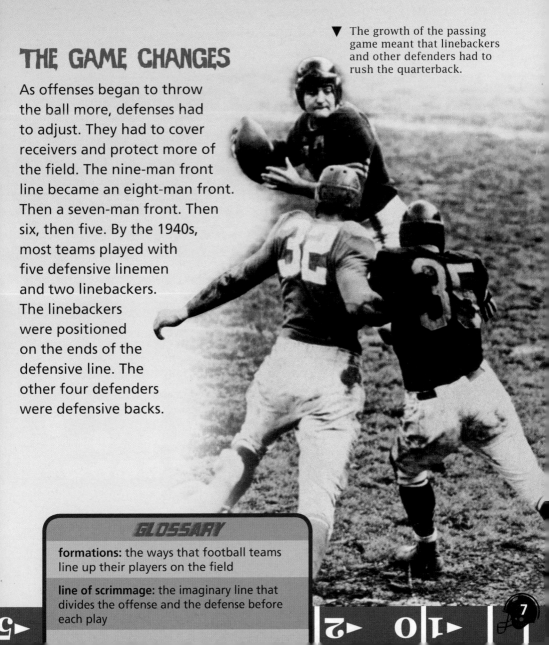

▼ The growth of the passing game meant that linebackers and other defenders had to rush the quarterback.

GLOSSARY

formations: the ways that football teams line up their players on the field

line of scrimmage: the imaginary line that divides the offense and the defense before each play

A NEW WAY

In 1951, the Chicago Bears **drafted** Bill George. He soon became the team's middle guard on defense. The middle guard lined up directly across from the offensive center. After the ball was snapped, the two players would battle. Then the middle guard would drop back behind the line. George figured he would skip that first step. He dropped back as soon as the ball was snapped. In doing so, George "invented" the position of middle linebacker.

▼ Bill George changed the way linebackers play their position.

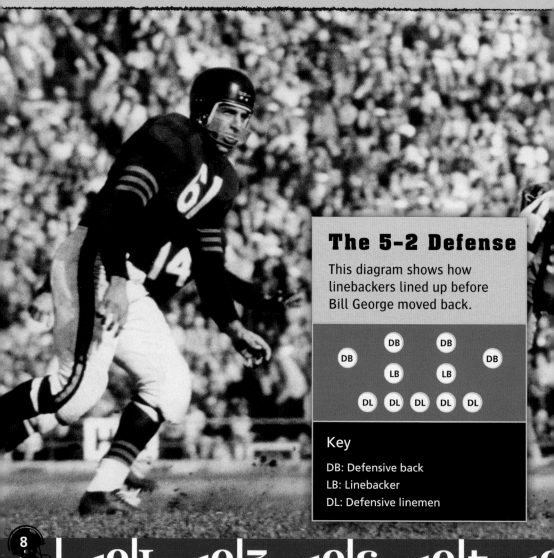

The 5-2 Defense

This diagram shows how linebackers lined up before Bill George moved back.

DB   DB

DB   DB

LB   LB

DL DL DL DL DL

Key

DB: Defensive back
LB: Linebacker
DL: Defensive linemen

▲ Chuck Bednarik (60) of the
Philadelphia Eagles was one of the
first great middle linebackers.

OTHERS FOLLOW SUIT

The truth is, George was probably not the first player to drop
back to play middle linebacker. But he was the first to have great
success at it. Soon every team began putting a man in the middle
behind the line of scrimmage. The 4–3 defense was born. The
"3" stands for the number of linebackers. With no one directly
blocking him, the middle linebacker was free to go find the ball
carrier. Middle linebackers became the stars of the defense.

GLOSSARY

drafted: selected from the top
college football players

▲ Bob Matheson (53) took the linebacker position in yet another direction.

3-4 OR 4-3?

In 1972, the Miami Dolphins became the first (and still only) NFL team to finish a season undefeated. The strength of their team was the 53 Defense. The key to that defense was having defensive end Bob Matheson stand up before the play. He played like a linebacker. Suddenly, Miami had a 3–4 defense: three defensive linemen and four linebackers. Today, however, most teams have gone back to playing the 4–3 defense.

Numbers Game

The name of the Dolphins 53 Defense had nothing to do with how the players lined up. Instead, it was Bob Matheson's uniform number.

A GIANT SUPERSTAR

In 1981, the New York Giants selected linebacker Lawrence Taylor with the second pick of the NFL Draft. "LT" changed the linebacker position forever. He was an incredible pass rusher and a terrific tackler. He excelled in pass coverage, too. No linebacker had ever messed up an offensive team's game plan like LT did! After Taylor came along, outside linebackers became the new stars of the defense.

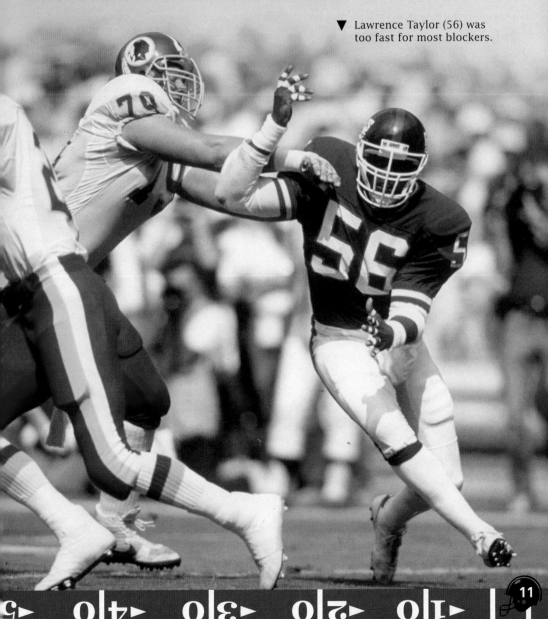

▼ Lawrence Taylor (56) was too fast for most blockers.

Stars of the Past

Here are some of the best linebackers in the history of pro football.

NATIONAL CELEBRITY

Sam Huff of the New York Giants was one of the most famous football players of the 1950s and 1960s. He was one of the first pro football players to be featured on the cover of *Time* magazine. In 1960, a television network aired a special called *The Violent World of Sam Huff*. Huff was mostly known for his big collisions with ball carriers. He was a great defender in pass coverage, too. He had 30 career **interceptions**.

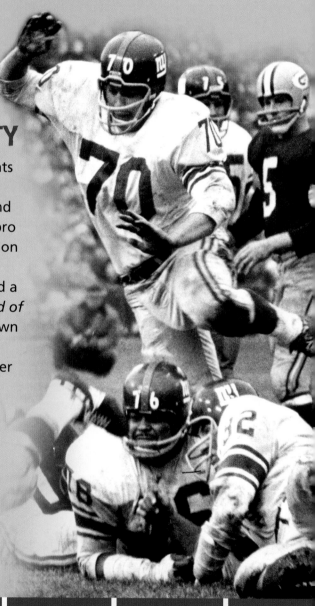

▶ Sam Huff (70) let nothing get in his way as he chased a ball carrier.

CONCRETE CHARLIE

Chuck Bednarik of the Philadelphia Eagles was so tough that his nickname was "Concrete Charlie." He played offense *and* defense. In the 1930s and 1940s, a lot of players did that. But Bednarik was still doing it in the 1950s! He was a great center on offense as well as a great linebacker. That earned him another nickname: "The Last of the 60-Minute Men." Bednarik was on the field for nearly all 60 minutes of game time.

▼ Chuck Bednarik takes down Frank Gifford of the New York Giants. The hit was so hard that it knocked Gifford out of football for a year!

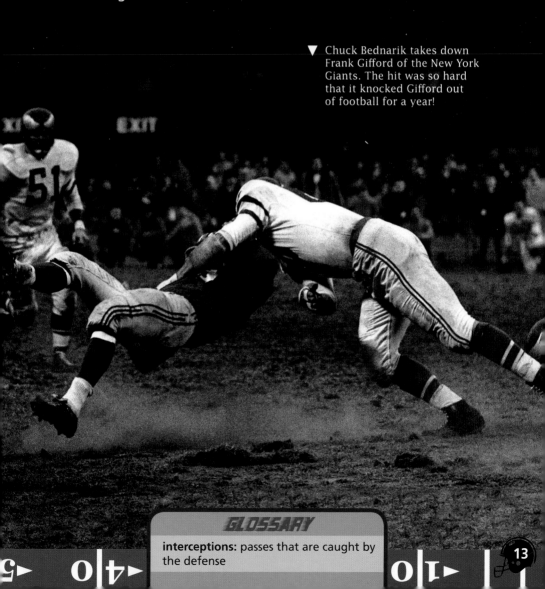

GLOSSARY

interceptions: passes that are caught by the defense

BIG BAD BEAR

Whenever experts talk about the roughest, toughest football players, the name Dick Butkus always comes up. Butkus followed Bill George at middle linebacker in Chicago. George was great, but Butkus may have been even better. Butkus played nine seasons (1965–1973) but was slowed by knee injuries. Still, this fierce tackler is considered one of the all-time greats.

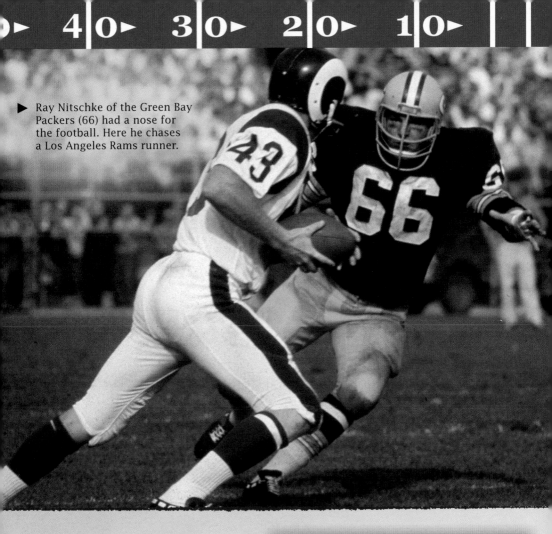

▶ Ray Nitschke of the Green Bay Packers (66) had a nose for the football. Here he chases a Los Angeles Rams runner.

PACKERS LEGEND

Ray Nitschke wore glasses that made him look like a mild-mannered librarian. But that didn't fool anybody who saw him play on Sundays. Once he stepped onto the field, he turned into a fearsome tackling machine. He was the leader of the Packers defense in the 1960s. He helped Green Bay win five NFL championships.

Ready for Contact

Willie Lanier's nickname was "Contact" because he always made solid contact with opposing ball carriers. Lanier was the middle linebacker for the Kansas City Chiefs in the 1960s and 1970s. If he wasn't making tackles, Lanier was causing **turnovers**. He had 27 interceptions and 18 fumble recoveries.

GLOSSARY

turnovers: interceptions or fumbles that are recovered by the defense

MAN OF STEEL

It's no coincidence that Jack Lambert's first season in Pittsburgh was the first year that the Steelers won the Super Bowl. That was in 1974, when Lambert was the NFL Defensive **Rookie** of the Year. Pittsburgh went on to win three more Super Bowls in the 1970s. Lambert was the man in the middle for "the Steel Curtain" defense each of those years.

▼ Jack Lambert (58) teams with other members of Pittsburgh's "Steel Curtain" to bring down a Baltimore Colts runner.

THE EYES HAVE IT

Mike Singletary was so **intense** that his eyes looked as if they would pop out of his head before every play! They would dart right, then left, and then straight ahead. Nothing escaped his attention. His intensity carried over to the whole Bears team in the 1980s. Chicago won Super Bowl XX because of its fearsome defense, led by Singletary.

Sack Master

By the 1980s, linebackers had become big parts of the pass rush. The best was Derrick Thomas of the Kansas City Chiefs. He used speed and great moves to get around blockers. In a 1990 game, he set an all-time record with seven **sacks**!

GLOSSARY

rookie: a player in his first season of pro football

intense: having great focus or concentration

sacks: tackles of the quarterback behind the line of scrimmage

Playing Linebacker

Linebackers need many different skills to succeed. Let's take a look at all of them.

INSIDE AND OUTSIDE

Most defenses have two outside linebackers. A 3–4 defense also has two inside linebackers. A 4–3 defense has only one linebacker on the inside. He is usually called a middle linebacker.

▶ DeMarcus Ware of the Dallas Cowboys plays outside linebacker. He watches the quarterback before the snap.

Outside linebackers stand with one foot behind the other. This helps them get a quick start when the ball is snapped.

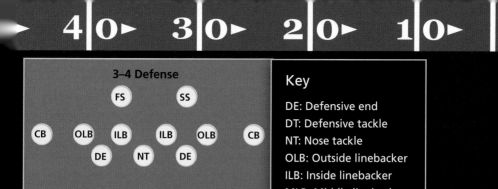

3–4 Defense

FS   SS

CB   OLB   ILB   ILB   OLB   CB

DE   NT   DE

4–3 Defense

FS   SS

CB   OLB   MLB   OLB   CB

DE   DT   DT   DE

Key

DE: Defensive end

DT: Defensive tackle

NT: Nose tackle

OLB: Outside linebacker

ILB: Inside linebacker

MLB: Middle linebacker

CB: Cornerback

FS: Free safety

SS: Strong safety

▼ A.J. Hawk of the Green Bay Packers plays inside linebacker. He often lines up opposite the quarterback.

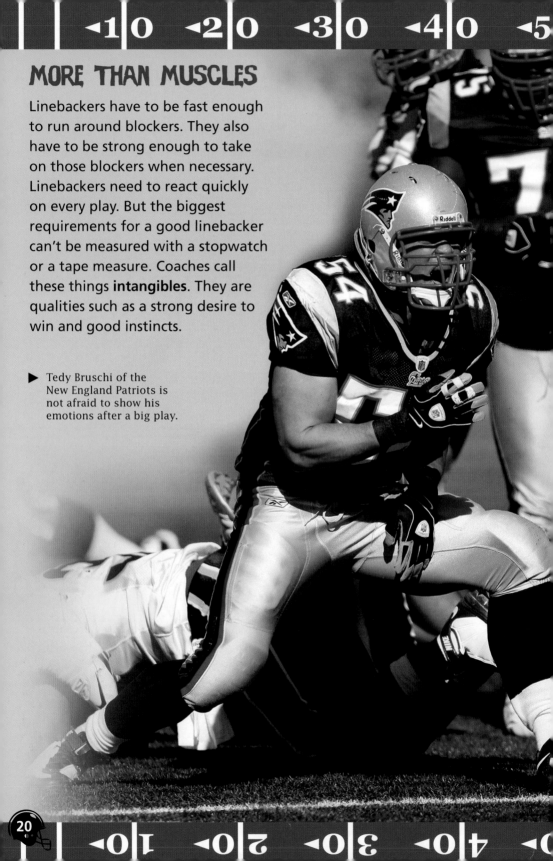

MORE THAN MUSCLES

Linebackers have to be fast enough to run around blockers. They also have to be strong enough to take on those blockers when necessary. Linebackers need to react quickly on every play. But the biggest requirements for a good linebacker can't be measured with a stopwatch or a tape measure. Coaches call these things **intangibles**. They are qualities such as a strong desire to win and good instincts.

▶ Tedy Bruschi of the New England Patriots is not afraid to show his emotions after a big play.

ONE SIZE DOESN'T FIT ALL

Some linebackers are best at rushing the passer from the outside. Some are best at stuffing the run inside. Because they do so many different things, linebackers come in different shapes and sizes. Outside linebackers are usually tall because they play opposite tall tackles and tight ends. Inside linebackers are shorter and heavier. Their main job is defending against the run.

► Seattle Seahawks linebacker Julian Peterson uses his height and speed to track down a Miami Dolphins running back.

GLOSSARY

intangibles: qualities that cannot be measured

21

FILM SCHOOL

NFL players watch a lot of video—of themselves! They also watch film of their opponents. Linebackers spend more time in the video room than other defensive players. They study the offense's formations. They want to know when the other team likes to pass the ball and when it likes to run. Linebackers know so much about their opponents that they are almost like extra coaches on the field.

▼ Linebacker Patrick Willis (52) of the San Francisco 49ers learns from the best. His coach, Mike Singletary (right), was a great linebacker. Together, they study the team's plays.

TEAM LEADERS

Here's another thing that linebackers have in common with coaches: They are born leaders. When a team needs a big play on defense, it almost always looks to a linebacker to step up. When players need a word of encouragement, it's often a linebacker who is the most vocal. Even off the field, linebackers are often the players that teammates look to for leadership.

◄ Ray Lewis of the Baltimore Ravens (52) celebrates a fumble recovery. Few players are better at firing up their teammates than Lewis.

23

TOP TACKLERS

A linebacker's main job is to stop the player with the ball. Many NFL defensive **schemes** are designed so that linebackers make most of the tackles. Often, the job of the defensive linemen is to take on blockers along the offensive line. That leaves linebackers free to stop the ball carrier.

▲ James Harrison (92) of the Pittsburgh Steelers prepares to tackle LaDainian Tomlinson of the San Diego Chargers. Harrison stays low, with an eye toward tackling the runner around the legs.

ON THE BLOCK

Of course, a linebacker still has to learn how to get past blockers. Sometimes, those blockers are big offensive linemen. Other times, a strong fullback leads the runner into a **hole**. A linebacker sheds, or gets past, a blocker either by strength, technique, or a combination of the two. The tricky part is trying to avoid blockers while keeping his eyes on the ball carrier!

▼ Brian Urlacher (54) of the Chicago Bears uses his strength and speed to get past two blockers.

GLOSSARY

schemes: plans

hole: an open area created by blockers into which a ball carrier can run

PROPER TECHNIQUE

A tackler should always bend at the knees, not the waist. He drives his chest into the ball carrier, wraps his arms around the runner, and lifts. A good tackler always keeps his head up. If he looks down at the ground, his neck could get injured. Also, he never uses his helmet to hit a player.

▼ James Farrior (51) of the Pittsburgh Steelers shows excellent tackling technique as he takes down a Baltimore Ravens runner.

The Stats Don't Lie

Tackles are not an official NFL statistic. Every team keeps track of its own tackle stats during a review of game film. On just about every team every year, a linebacker leads his team in tackles.

SIDELINE TO SIDELINE

Linebackers must never give up on a play. They have to follow the ball wherever it goes. If a ball carrier runs to one side and then switches back to the other, the linebacker has to follow quickly. That's called pursuing the play. Linebackers have to play sideline to sideline. They don't stay on one side of the field. They go wherever the action is.

▲ Arizona Cardinals linebacker Karlos Dansby (58) chases down a Philadelphia Eagles running back.

Playing the Pass

In today's NFL, linebackers have more work to do in pass coverage than ever before. Linebackers need to be able to keep up with talented receivers. They also cover running backs or tight ends.

SNAP JUDGMENT

► DeMeco Ryans of the Houston Texans watches the quarterback as he drops back into pass coverage.

On every play, a linebacker has to make a split-second decision: Play the run or play the pass. Sounds easy, right? Well, many times a quarterback tries to trick the linebackers with a **play-action pass**. The quarterback fakes a handoff to a running back and hides the ball on his hip. A good play-action fake by a quarterback can "freeze" the linebacker just long enough to allow a receiver to get past him.

Linebackers need good footwork. They stay on their toes as they drop into pass coverage.

THE PASS ROUTES

All receivers run the same basic **routes**. A linebacker who has studied a lot of film knows what types of routes the receiver he is covering runs most often. Most linebackers are assigned to cover running backs and tight ends when they go out for passes.

Zone or Man?

Teams have two basic types of pass defense: zone or man-for-man. In a zone defense, a linebacker is assigned to cover a certain area of the field. In man-for-man defense, he covers a specific player.

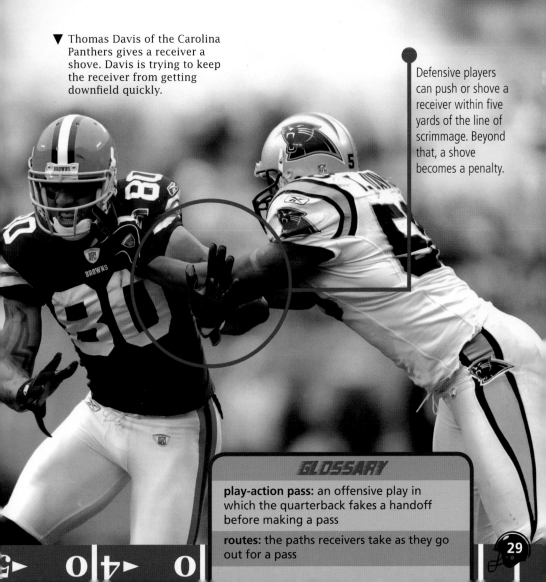

▼ Thomas Davis of the Carolina Panthers gives a receiver a shove. Davis is trying to keep the receiver from getting downfield quickly.

Defensive players can push or shove a receiver within five yards of the line of scrimmage. Beyond that, a shove becomes a penalty.

GLOSSARY

play-action pass: an offensive play in which the quarterback fakes a handoff before making a pass

routes: the paths receivers take as they go out for a pass

STICK WITH THE RECEIVER

In man-for-man coverage, a linebacker has to stick with the receiver. He can't hold that player. He has to run with him. That often means backpedaling or running sideways. He watches the receiver's eyes to know when the ball is in the air. In zone coverage, a linebacker follows the quarterback's eyes to see where he will throw the ball.

The linebacker tries to keep himself between the quarterback and the receiver.

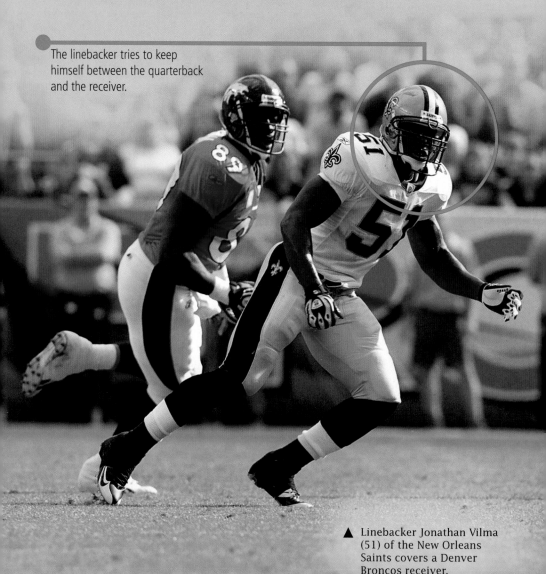

▲ Linebacker Jonathan Vilma (51) of the New Orleans Saints covers a Denver Broncos receiver.

KNOCK IT DOWN!

When a pass is thrown, the linebacker tries to keep the receiver from catching it. He can't hit or push the receiver before the ball arrives. But he can knock the ball away. He might even be able to catch the pass. An interception can be a game-changing play.

▲ Tedy Bruschi of the Patriots arrives in time to knock the ball away from a San Diego Chargers receiver.

Great Pickers

A "pick" is another name for an interception. Kansas City's Donnie Edwards and Baltimore's Ray Lewis have the most picks among active linebackers. Through 2008, they each have intercepted 28 passes.

Rushing the Passer

Linebackers don't always drop back into pass coverage, of course. Sometimes, they go after the quarterback.

SACK ARTISTS

When a linebacker rushes the passer, the play is called a **blitz**. Some outside linebackers excel at rushing the passer. Making a sack is always a big play for a defense. It puts the offense farther back. Even getting near the passer can cause trouble. If a quarterback throws the ball quickly to escape a linebacker, the pass is probably going to be a bad one.

▶ Jarret Johnson of the Baltimore Ravens sets his sight on quarterback Eli Manning of the New York Giants.

HOW THEY DO IT

Linebackers depend on speed to reach the passer. They get a running start and try to burst around blockers. If they are blocked, they use their arms to push the blockers back toward the passer. They can also use their strength to push blockers aside. If that happens, the quarterback had better watch out!

▼ James Farrior of the Steelers sacks quarterback Donovan McNabb of the Philadelphia Eagles.

GLOSSARY

blitz: a rush of the quarterback by linebackers or defensive backs

Stars of Today

We know what makes a good linebacker. Now let's meet some of the best in today's NFL.

BIG PLAYMAKER

James Harrison of the Pittsburgh Steelers had a great 2008 season. He had 16 sacks and was named the NFL's Defensive Player of the Year. The regular season was nothing, however, compared to what he did in the Super Bowl. On the last play of the first half, he picked off a pass by Kurt Warner of the Arizona Cardinals. Harrison then rumbled 100 yards for a touchdown!

► James Harrison is about to cross the goal line on his super play in the Super Bowl!

THE NEXT BUTKUS?

When he was in college at Mississippi, Patrick Willis won
the Butkus Award. Each year, the award goes to the best
linebacker in college football. The award is named for
all-time great Dick Butkus. Now Willis is in the NFL with
the San Francisco 49ers. He hopes to follow in Butkus's
footsteps as one of the best NFL linebackers ever.

▼ Patrick Willis (52) of the San
Francisco 49ers always seems
to be near the football.

▲ DeMarcus Ware (94) of the Dallas Cowboys wraps up another sack.

ALL-AROUND PLAYER

DeMarcus Ware was a top pass rusher in college as a defensive end at Troy State. But the Dallas Cowboys drafted him in 2005 and turned him into a linebacker. He quickly showed he can do more than just rush the passer. In 2008, Ware led the NFL with 20 sacks and made the **Pro Bowl**.

GLOSSARY

Pro Bowl: the NFL's annual all-star game

ANOTHER CHICAGO GREAT

They don't call the Chicago Bears "the Monsters of the Midway" for nothing! Chicago always seems to have a great defense. And that defense always seems to be led by the team's linebackers. The Bears' middle linebackers get most of the attention, but the outside linebackers can be pretty good, too. Lance Briggs is one of those guys. He made the Pro Bowl after the 2005, 2006, and 2008 seasons.

◀ Lance Briggs (55) is fast enough to cover receivers from sideline to sideline.

Tale of Two Cities

Julian Peterson is a two-city star. With San Francisco, he made the Pro Bowl twice. In 2006, Peterson joined the Seattle Seahawks, San Francisco's rival. He made the Pro Bowl for his new team, too.

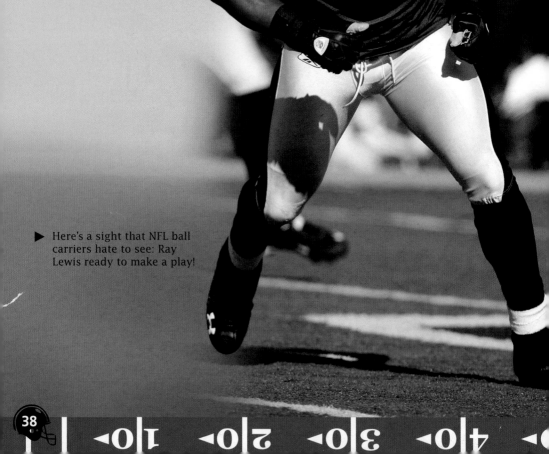

EMOTIONAL LEADER

Ray Lewis has been the heart and soul of the Baltimore Ravens defense ever since the team's first season in 1996. He is a vocal leader who really knows how to get his team pumped up. In 2000, Lewis was the NFL Defensive Player of the Year. He was also named Most Valuable Player (MVP) of Baltimore's win over the New York Giants in Super Bowl XXXV.

▶ Here's a sight that NFL ball carriers hate to see: Ray Lewis ready to make a play!

ALL-AROUND TALENT

Bill George. Dick Butkus. Mike Singletary. The Chicago Bears have had some great middle linebackers. Today, Brian Urlacher is carrying on that tradition. Urlacher is an amazing athlete. In college he didn't just play linebacker. He sometimes lined up at safety on defense, wide receiver on offense, and was a return man on **special teams**!

Lights Out

Shawne Merriman's nickname is "Lights Out." Why? The lights go out for opposing ball carriers when he hits them! Merriman plays for the San Diego Chargers. He was the NFL Defensive Rookie of the Year for 2005. He led the league with 17 sacks the following season.

GLOSSARY

special teams: the groups of players who are on the field during kicks and punts

CHAPTER
5

Future Star: You!

Would you like to be a linebacker? Here are some good ways to practice key skills.

RUNNING BACKWARD

Linebackers have to move quickly from side to side to follow the play. To practice your footwork, set up with your feet apart. At a signal, shuffle to one side and then the other. Try not to cross your feet. Instead, bring them together quickly and then push off to one side with one foot. Stay slightly crouched, with your chest over your knees.

▼ As you do this drill, keep your head up and your eyes forward, even as you move your body from side to side.

READ AND REACT

Linebackers have to get past blockers quickly. Here's an easy drill you can do to practice this skill. Set up opposite a friend, who is the offensive lineman. Count "1–2–3–hike!" Try to burst past the lineman or push your way past to one side or the other. The offensive lineman is supposed to keep his hands in front. Don't push too hard or knock each other over. The key is the quickness you use to react to the "hike."

▶ The player in yellow shows how linebackers can use their hands to get past blockers.

Warning!

Don't try tackling until you have proper safety equipment and are supervised by a coach. The football players you see on TV wear helmets and a lot of padding. They have also learned the proper way to tackle from a coach.

GETTING BACK IN COVERAGE

Running backward with a receiver is an important linebacker skill. Line up opposite a friend who is the receiver. At the snap of the ball, start backpedaling. Turn and run with the receiver if he gets too close. Stay as close as you can to the receiver without touching him. See the photo on page 28 for an example on how to move back quickly and smoothly.

Watch and See

When you can't get out and play football, find a game on television. When you tune in, try to follow the linebackers. Watch what they do when the offense runs or passes. Pay attention when the announcers talk about the linebackers, too. Many announcers are former players. They can help you understand the things you need to know about playing linebacker. You can learn a lot just by watching and listening!

USE YOUR FRIENDS

Here's a game you can play with two friends. One friend is the quarterback, and the other is the receiver. You be the linebacker. Have the quarterback secretly call a pass route for the receiver. See if you can break up the pass or even intercept it. Take turns, with everybody getting a try at each position. Remember, though, no tackling!

Record Book

Who's the best of the best? Here are the top five linebackers in some key categories.

Sacks, Career
1. Kevin Greene: 157.0
2. Lawrence Taylor: 132.5
3. Derrick Thomas: 126.5
4. Rickey Jackson: 115.0
5. Andre Tippett: 100.0

Note: Greene also had three sacks as a defensive end; Jackson had 13 sacks as a defensive end.

Sacks, Season
1. Lawrence Taylor, Giants: 20.5 (1986)
2. Derrick Thomas, Chiefs: 20 (1990)
   DeMarcus Ware, Cowboys: 20 (2008)
4. Andre Tippett, Patriots: 18.5 (1984)
5. Joey Porter, Dolphins: 17.5 (2008)

▲ Kevin Greene (91) used his speed to record sacks for the Rams, Steelers, Panthers, and 49ers.

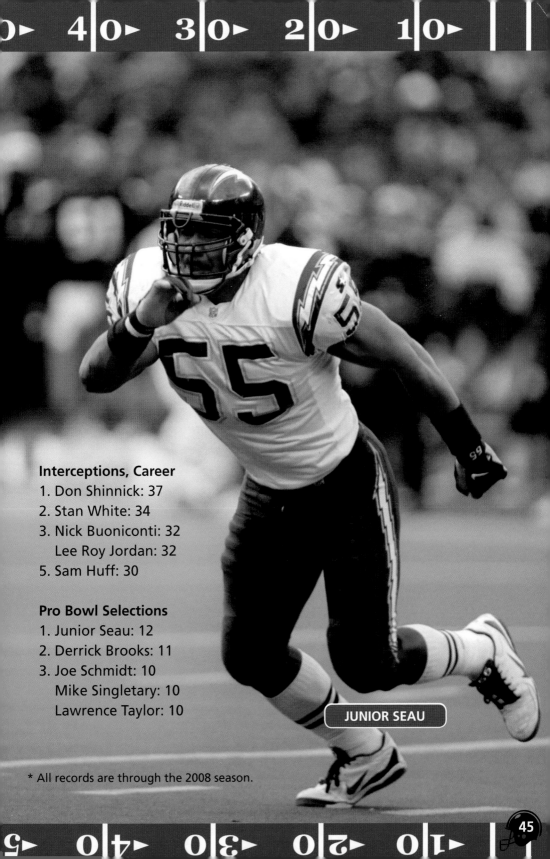

Interceptions, Career
1. Don Shinnick: 37
2. Stan White: 34
3. Nick Buoniconti: 32
   Lee Roy Jordan: 32
5. Sam Huff: 30

Pro Bowl Selections
1. Junior Seau: 12
2. Derrick Brooks: 11
3. Joe Schmidt: 10
   Mike Singletary: 10
   Lawrence Taylor: 10

JUNIOR SEAU

* All records are through the 2008 season.

Glossary

blitz: a rush of the quarterback by linebackers or defensive backs

drafted: selected from the top college football players

formations: the ways that football teams line up their players on the field

hole: an open area created by blockers into which a ball carrier can run

intangibles: qualities that cannot be measured

intense: having great focus or concentration

interception: a pass that is caught by the defense

line of scrimmage: the imaginary line that divides the offense and the defense before each play

play-action pass: an offensive play in which the quarterback fakes a handoff before making a pass

Pro Bowl: the NFL's annual all-star game

rookie: a player in his first season of pro football

routes: the paths receivers take as they go out for a pass

sacks: tackles of the quarterback behind the line of scrimmage

schemes: plans

special teams: the groups of players who are on the field during kicks and punts

turnovers: interceptions or fumbles that are recovered by the defense

Find Out More

Books

Buckley, James, Jr. *Eyewitness Football*. New York: DK Publishing, 1999

Polzer, Tim. *Play Football!* New York: DK Publishing, 2003

Stewart, Mark. *The Ultimate 10: Football*. Pleasantville, N.Y.: Gareth Stevens, 2009.

Web Sites

www.nfl.com

The official web site of the National Football League is packed with stats, video, news, and player biographies. Football fans can find all they need to know about their favorite players and teams here.

www.nflrush.com

Check out the official kids' site of the NFL. Meet star players, see video of great plays, and get tips from the pros!

Publisher's note to educators and parents: Our editors have carefully reviewed these web sites to ensure that they are suitable for children. Many web sites change frequently, however, and we cannot guarantee that a site's future contents will continue to meet our high standards of quality and educational value. Be advised that children should be closely supervised whenever they access the Internet.

Index

About the Author

Jim Gigliotti is a freelance writer who lives in southern California with his wife and two children. A former editor at NFL Publishing, he has written more than two dozen books for youngsters and adults, including *Stadium Stories: USC Trojans* and kids' titles on football stars Tom Brady, Peyton Manning, and LaDainian Tomlinson.